# ANIMALS IN HEBREW
# A DAY AT THE ZOO

## A Story In Rhymes For English Speaking Kids

By Sarah Mazor

Illustrations by Benny Rahdiana

## In This Book

- Publisher's Note
- Guide to Transliteration of Hebrew Words
- Animals in Hebrew: A Day at the Zoo
- An Illustrated Summary Chart of the Animals in the Book

*Extras:*

- More About Animals' Hebrew Names
- The Animals in Feminine Form: In English, In Hebrew and in Transliteration
- The Animals in Plural Form: In English, In Hebrew and in Transliteration
- Bonus Hebrew Words Relating to a Visit at the Zoo with English Transliteration and Translation

Copyright © 2014 Sarah Mazor
MazorBooks
All rights reserved.
ISBN-13: 978-1505580020
ISBN-10: 1505580021

## Publisher's Note

MazorBooks is delighted to present its fourth installment in the 'A Taste of Hebrew' series for English speaking kids.

*ANIMALS IN HEBREW: A Day at the Zoo*

Read about Ami and Tami's visit to the zoo and learn the Hebrew names for many animals, including the lion, the tiger, the giraffe, and many more.

Please note that male pronouns are used in the text corresponding to the male name for animals. In cases where the Hebrew names are the same for the male and the female animals (i.e. zehbra, tzipor), the pronoun 'it' is used.

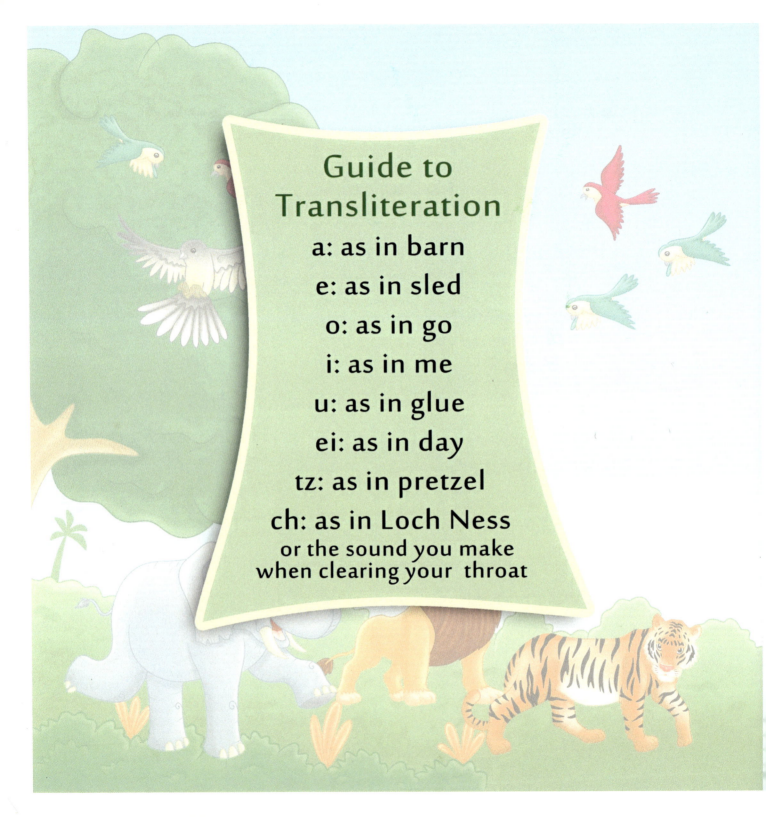

Ami and Tami
Their mom and dad too
Decided to spend
A day at the zoo

A fun day that's filled
With laughter and games
And learning the Hebrew
For animals' names

*Arye* the mighty lion and a royal dude
Thinks it's not for him to hunt around for food
His loud blaring roar tells all that he feels
Others must provide all his daily meals

*Namer* the stripy tiger the biggest of cats
Feasts on pigs and deer not just milk and rats
Powerful and strong and a speedy fellow
He also can be loud just listen to him bellow

*Pil* the elephant gentle and smart
Has a huge brain and a very big heart
To satisfy his hunger *Pil* eats tons of hay
Keeping him busy most of the day

*Dov* the burly bear loves to socialize
To play with other bears no matter their size
He also likes to eat all kinds of meats
And fruits and veggies and other yummy treats

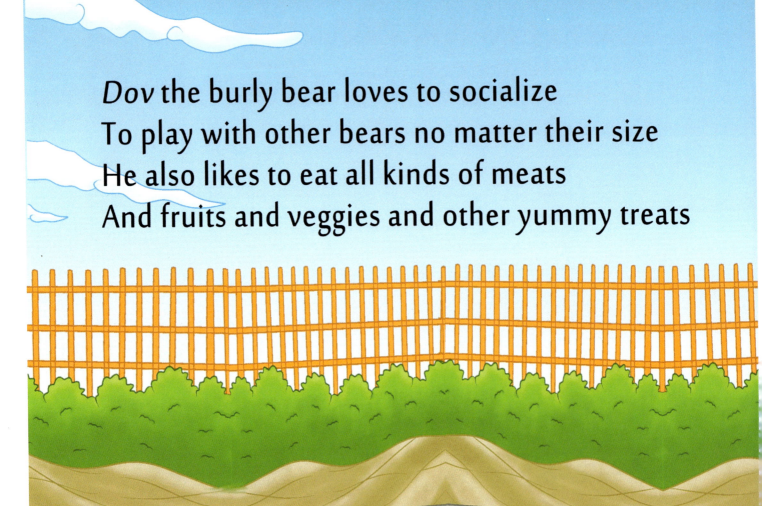
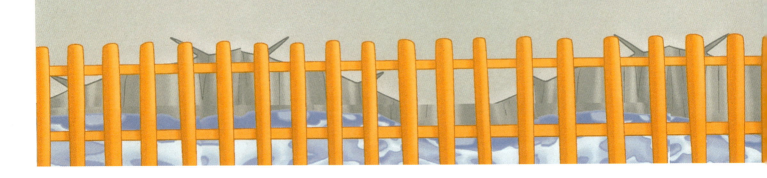

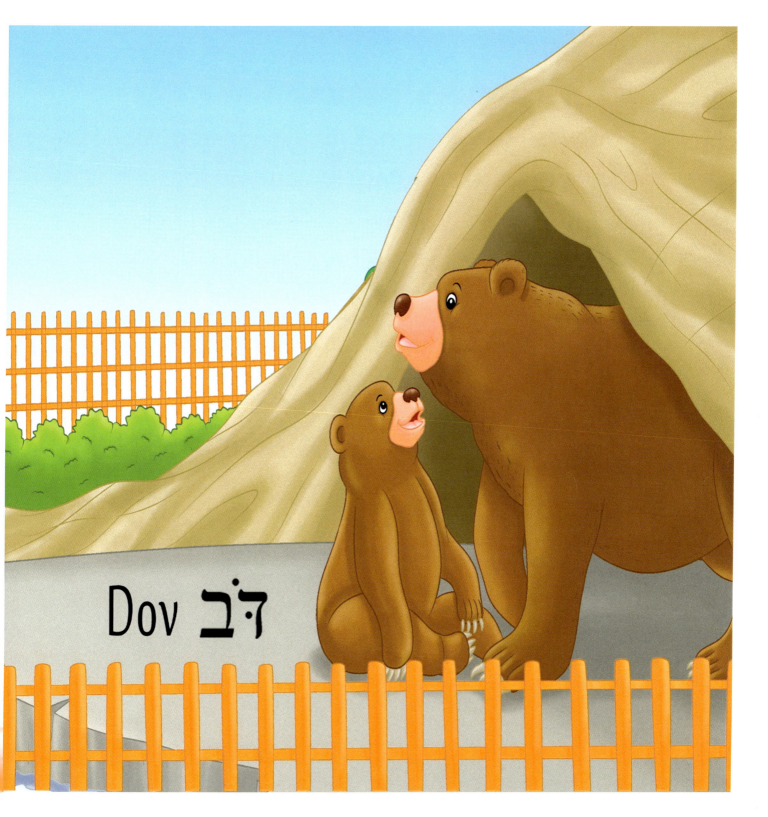

*Nachash* the snake has no eyelids or nose
No ears on its head no legs and no toes
It smells with its tongue its eyes never close
It crawls on its belly wherever it goes

נָחָשׁ
Nachash

*Kof* the agile monkey loves to climb and swing
Up and down branch to branch never tiring
*Kof* enjoys the taste of fruit and other plants
Sometimes he will dig for termites and for ants

*Giraf* the giraffe already at birth
Is taller than most creatures on earth
*Giraf* eats all day tree leaves and shoots
Flowers and buds and seasonal fruits

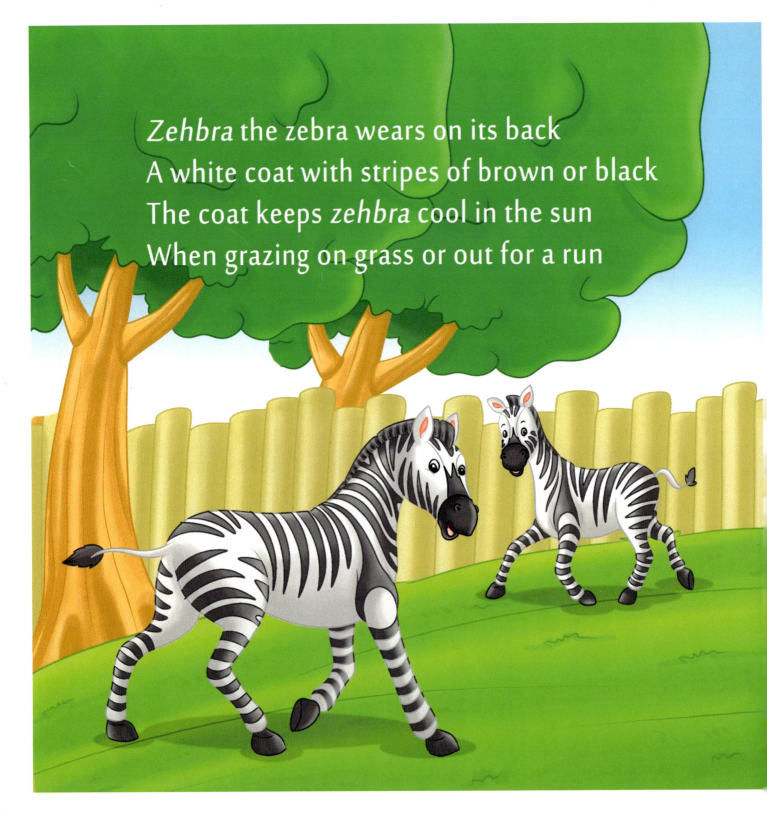

*Zehbra* the zebra wears on its back
A white coat with stripes of brown or black
The coat keeps *zehbra* cool in the sun
When grazing on grass or out for a run

*Tzipor* the bird lets us know how it feels
It chirps and it quacks it tweedles and trills
All birds have wings but some cannot fly
Like penguins that never take off to the sky

צִפּוֹר
Tzipor

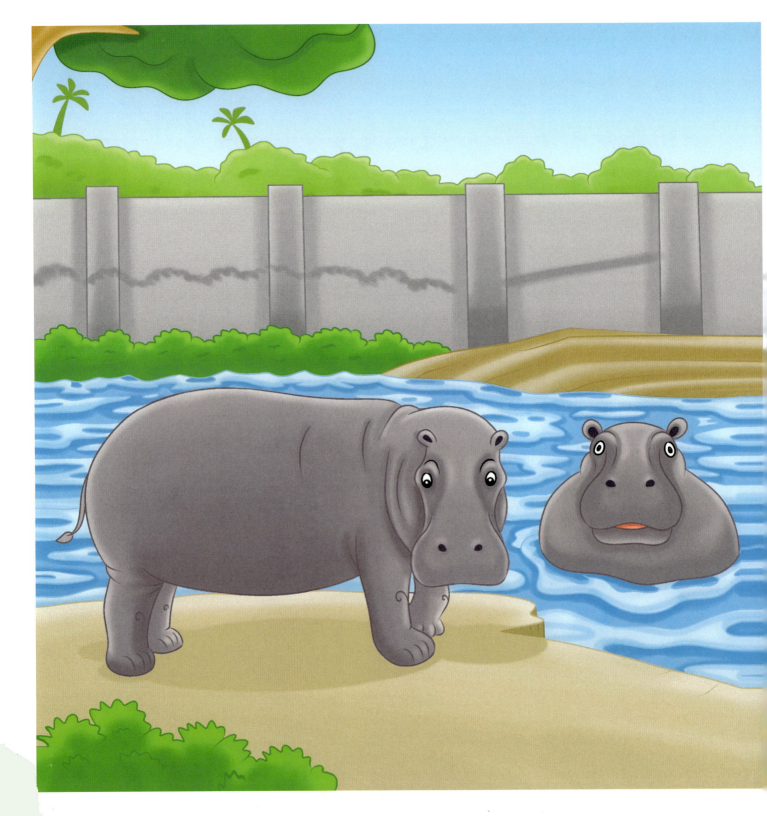

*Hipopotam* the hippo spends most of its time
In swamps and in lakes covered in slime
Though seemingly lazy and big and so fat
It can run a mile in three minutes flat

הִיפּוֹפּוֹטָם
Hipopotam

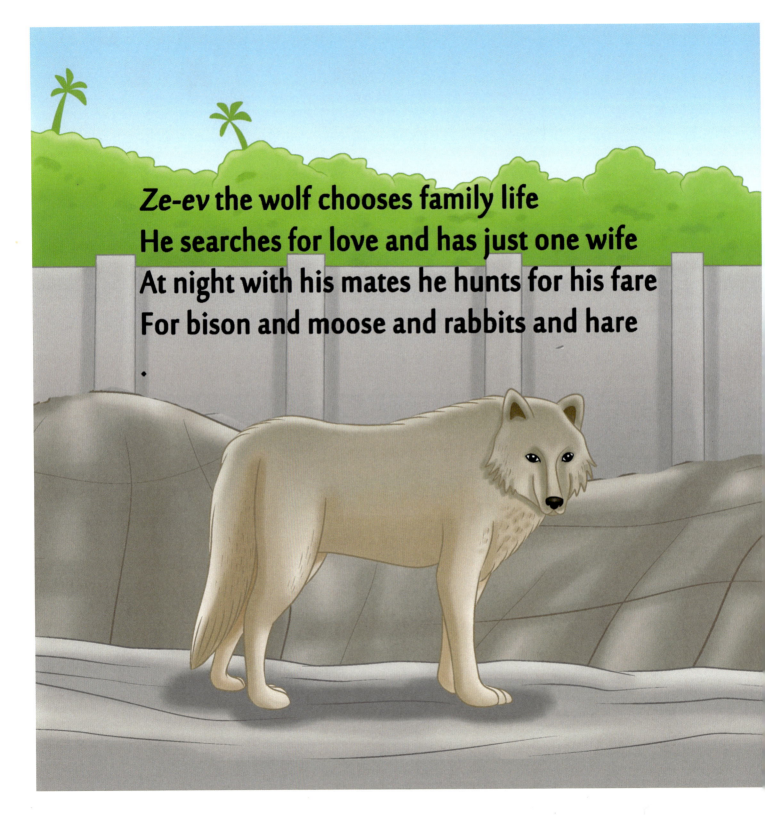

*Ze-ev the wolf chooses family life*
*He searches for love and has just one wife*
At night with his mates he hunts for his fare
For bison and moose and rabbits and hare

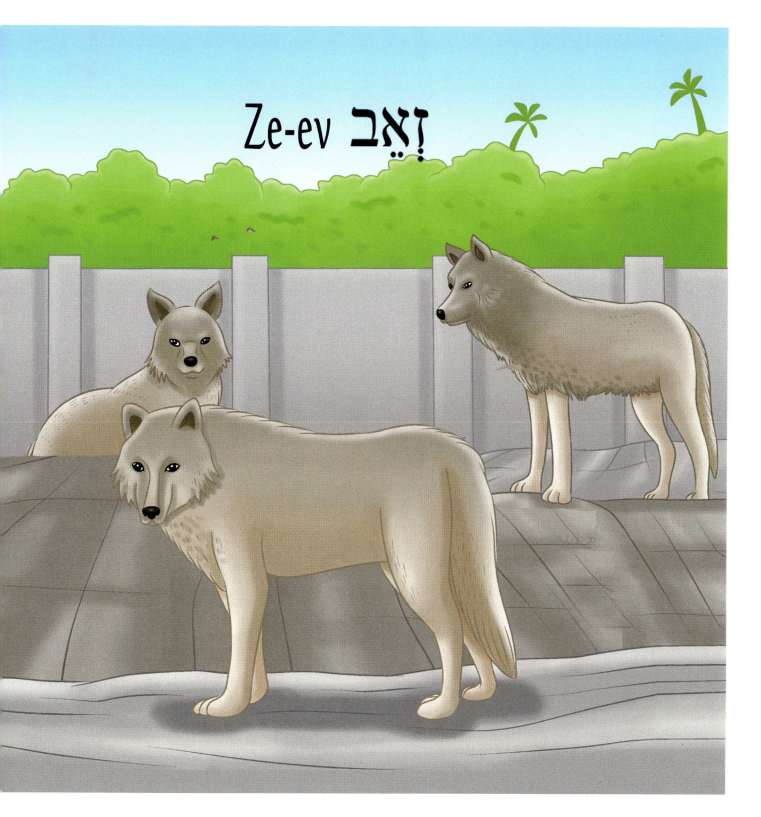

*Shu-al* the fox hides in the day
At night he goes solo in search of small prey
The cunning *Shu-al* wisely conceals
His leftover food for later on meals

Ami and Tami
Their mom and dad too
Had a great time
That day in the zoo

A fun day it was
Full of laughter and games
And saying in Hebrew
The animals' names

| | |
|---|---|
| **Arye is a Lion**<br>אַרְיֵה | **Namer is a Tiger**<br>נָמֵר |
| **Pil is an Elephant**<br>פִּיל | **Dov is a Bear**<br>דֹּב |

# More About Animals' Hebrew Names

- Many Modern Hebrew names for animals are biblical in origin, but not all. For example, the origin of *giraf* is Arabic and the origin of *hipopotam* is Latin.
- In the bible and in ancient Jewish texts the male and female animals are usually identified by the same name. In Modern Hebrew most animal names are distinctly male or female, but not all. For example, *tzipor* is the name for both the male and the female bird
- Most of the Hebrew names for female animals are based on their male counterpart. For example, *Pila* (f.) is based on *Pil* (m.), the elephant and *Levi-ah* (f.), a lioness, is derived from *lavi*, a synonym for *arye* (lion).

# The Animals In Hebrew Feminine Form
## In the order they appear in the book

| English | Transliteration | Hebrew |
|---|---|---|
| Lioness | Levi-ah | לְבִיאָה |
| Tigress | Nemera | נְמֵרָה |
| Elephant | Pila | פִּילָה |
| Bear | Duba | דֻּבָּה |
| Snake | Nachash* | נָחָשׁ* |
| Monkey | Kofa | קוֹפָה |
| Giraffe | Girafa | גִ'ירָפָה |
| Zebra | Zehbra | זֶבְרָה |
| Bird | Tzipor | צִפּוֹר |
| Hippo | Hipopotam | הִיפּוֹפּוֹטָם |
| Wolf | Ze-eva | זְאֵבָה |
| Fox | Shu-ala | שׁוּעָלָה |

* *Nachash* (נָחָשׁ) is commonly used for both male and female snakes, but *nechasha* (נְחָשָׁה) is also correct

# The Animals In Hebrew Plural Form
*In the order they appear in the book*

| English | Transliteration | Hebrew |
|---|---|---|
| Lions | Arayot | זֶבְרוֹת |
| Tigers | Nemerim | נְמֵרִים |
| Elephants | Pilim | פִּילִים |
| Bears | Dubim | דוּבִּים |
| Snakes | Nechashim | נְחָשִׁים |
| Monkeys | Kofim | קוֹפִים |
| Giraffes | Girafot | ג'ירָפוֹת |
| Zehbras | Zehbrot | זֶבְרוֹת |
| Birds | Tziporim | צִפּוֹרִים |
| Hippos | Hipopotamim | הִיפּוֹפּוֹטָמִים |
| Wolves | Ze-evim | זְאֵבִים |
| Foxes | Shu-alim | שׁוּעָלִים |

# Hebrew Words for A Day at the Zoo

| English | Transliteration | Hebrew |
|---|---|---|
| Animal | Chaya | חַיָּה |
| Animals | Chayot | חַיּוֹת |
| Zoo | Gan Chayot | גַּן חַיּוֹת |
| Ticket Booth | Kupa | קוּפָּה |
| Ticket | Kartis | כַּרְטִיס |
| Entrance | Knisa | כְּנִיסָה |
| Exit | Yetzi-ah | יְצִיאָה |

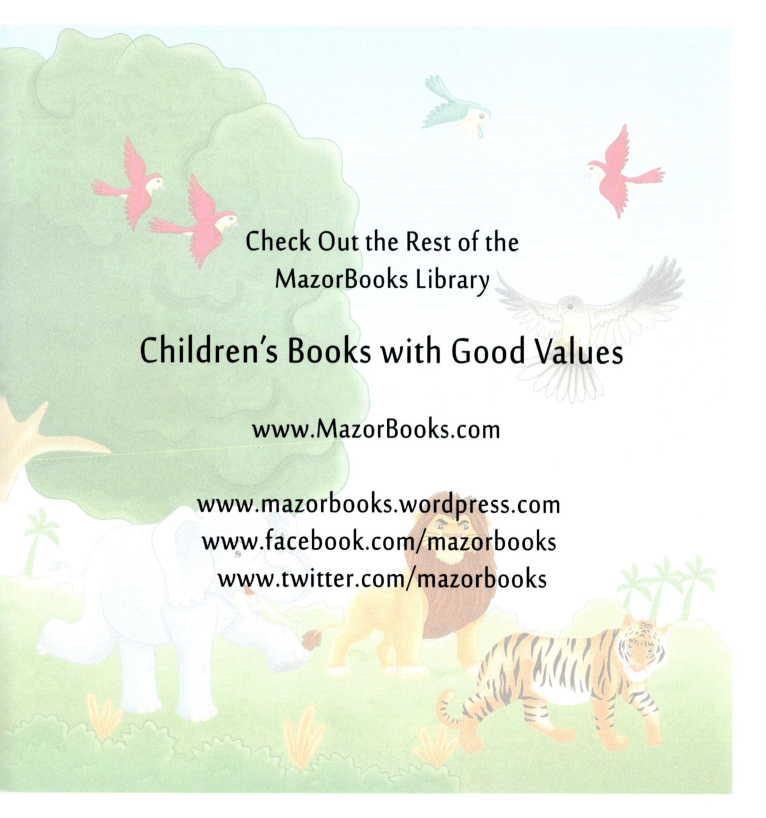

Check Out the Rest of the MazorBooks Library

## Children's Books with Good Values

www.MazorBooks.com

www.mazorbooks.wordpress.com
www.facebook.com/mazorbooks
www.twitter.com/mazorbooks

# A Taste of Hebrew
## For English Speaking Kids

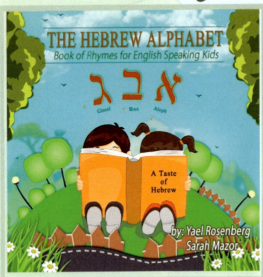
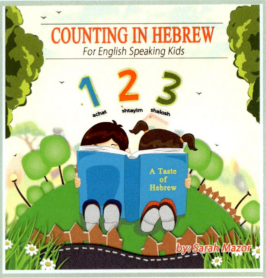
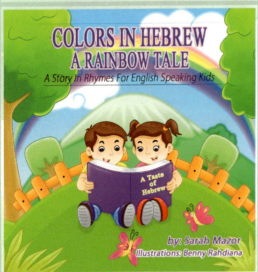
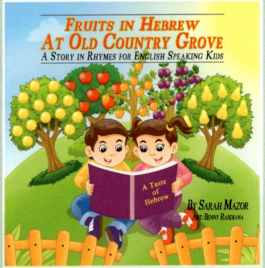

**(Available on Amazon and Barnes and Noble)**

Made in the USA
Columbia, SC
13 December 2019

84806119R00024